INSIDE GUIDES

INCREDIBLE PLANTS

Written by

BARBARA TAYLOR

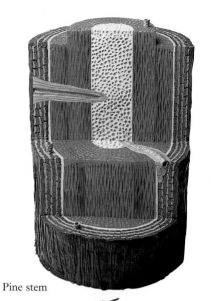

Pine stem

A DK PUBLISHING BOOK

Editor Kitty Blount
Art Editor Cormac Jordan
Managing editor Gillian Denton
Managing art editor Julia Harris
US Editor Camela Decaire
Editorial consultant Dr. Geoffrey Chapman
Picture Research Julia Harris-Voss
Production Charlotte Traill
Photography Geoff Brightling
Modelmaker Peter Minister Models

First American Edition, 1997
2 4 6 8 10 9 7 5 3 1
Published in the United States by
DK Publishing, Inc.
95 Madison Avenue
New York, New York 10016

Copyright © 1997
Dorling Kindersley Limited, London
Visit us on the World Wide Web at
http://www.dk.com

Published in Great Britain by Dorling Kindersley Ltd.

A CIP catalogue record for this book is
available from the Library of Congress.
ISBN 0751 3 54996

Reproduced in Italy by G.R.B. Graphica, Verona
Printed in Singapore by Toppan

Fly agaric
toadstool

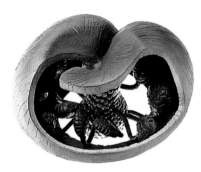

Spore release
in fern

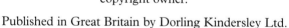

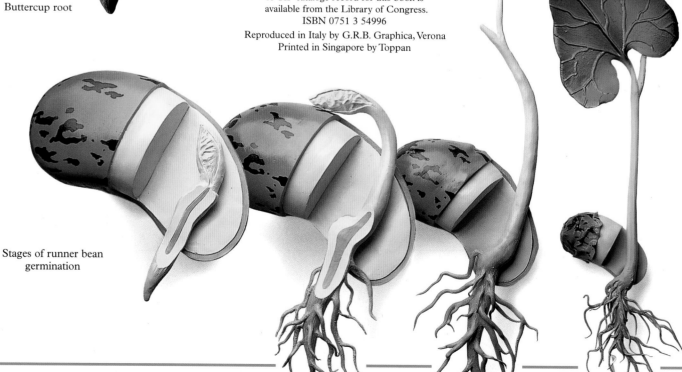

Buttercup root

Stages of runner bean
germination

Contents

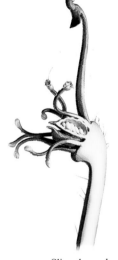

Inside a
monkshood
flower

Slice through
a monkshood
flower

Internal structure
of a chloroplast

Plants at work

Without plants, you would not be alive. Most plants can make their own food. Animals, including people, cannot do this. All animals have to eat plants, or eat animals that have eaten plants. Plants do many of the things animals do, such as feeding, breathing, reproducing, and growing. Unlike animals, plants keep growing throughout their lives. Although plants do not move around like animals, they do make small movements, and they use wind, water, or animals to disperse their pollen, seeds, and spores. There are more than 550,000 different kinds of plants in the world.

Flowers on the move
Cells send signals that control growth of the flower stalk, so the flower always faces the light.

Sun worshipers
Plants like this lesser celandine can move their flowers to face the sun as it moves across the sky. They sense the light using pigments in their cells.

Building blocks
Plants are made up of microscopic "boxes" of living material called cells. A cell takes in energy and uses this to build itself up and to reproduce. Some plants have only one cell, while more complex plants, such as trees, have many, many billions of cells.

Nucleus
The nucleus is the control center of the cell, rather like the cell's "brain."

Endoplasmic reticulum
This is a mazelike network of membranes that makes and stores chemical substances.

Cell wall
The cell wall is a jacket around the cell made of cellulose layers.

Cell shape
The cell walls are tough, which gives the cell a fixed shape.

Chloroplast
Food is made and stored in chloroplasts (pp. 10–11).

Cytoplasm
The cytoplasm is a jellylike substance that fills the space between the cell membrane and the nucleus.

Plant uses
From dyes, food, and medicines to fabrics, perfume, and furniture, people use plants in many different ways. For thousands of years, people have crushed plants such as saffron, lichens, woad, and heather to make dyes for fabrics and leather. This picture shows dye pits in Marakesh, Morocco.

Plasmodesmata
Threads of cytoplasm called plasmodesmata pass through the cell wall and link one cell to another. Plasmodesmata and cytoplasm are different colors in this model to make the image clearer.

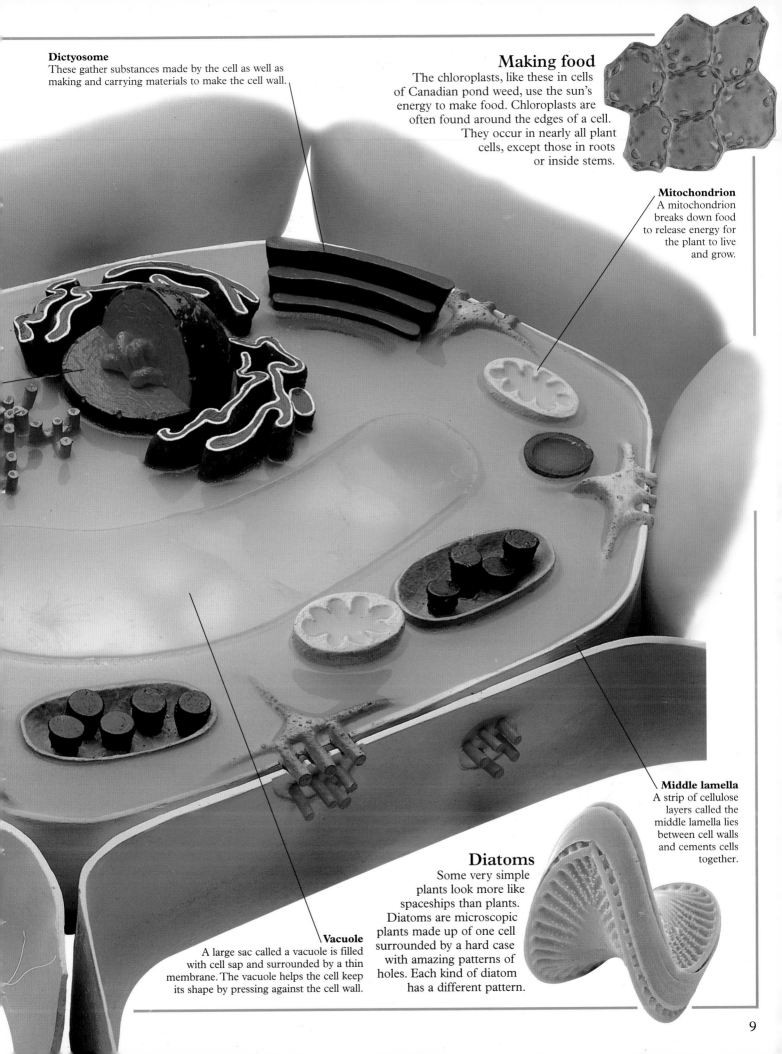

Dictyosome
These gather substances made by the cell as well as making and carrying materials to make the cell wall.

Making food
The chloroplasts, like these in cells of Canadian pond weed, use the sun's energy to make food. Chloroplasts are often found around the edges of a cell. They occur in nearly all plant cells, except those in roots or inside stems.

Mitochondrion
A mitochondrion breaks down food to release energy for the plant to live and grow.

Middle lamella
A strip of cellulose layers called the middle lamella lies between cell walls and cements cells together.

Diatoms
Some very simple plants look more like spaceships than plants. Diatoms are microscopic plants made up of one cell surrounded by a hard case with amazing patterns of holes. Each kind of diatom has a different pattern.

Vacuole
A large sac called a vacuole is filled with cell sap and surrounded by a thin membrane. The vacuole helps the cell keep its shape by pressing against the cell wall.

9

Leaf power

Leaves are living factories, making food from water and a gas called carbon dioxide. To fuel their task, leaves use the energy from sunlight, which they capture with a green pigment called chlorophyll. Leaves come in many shapes and sizes, but they are usually thin, flat, and arranged to catch as much light as possible. Some leaves have special features. Furry leaves keep out strong sunlight on mountains. Cactus leaves are narrow spines, stopping the plants from losing too much water in hot, dry places. The thick, waxy leaves of water plants encourage water to run off, preventing the plant from getting waterlogged.

Blood red
Herb Robert was used as a medicine for blood disorders and to heal cuts. Because it is red, the plant was associated with blood.

Autumn leaf
In autumn the leaves lose their chlorophyll and turn red all over.

Granum
Disk-shaped sacs called thylakoids are piled up like stacks of coins. One stack is called a granum.

Spangle gall
Spangle galls form when an oak leaf grows abnormally around wasp eggs laid inside it.

Leaf shapes
Herb Robert has compound leaves made up of several leaflets radiating from a leaf stalk, like fingers of a hand. Simple leaves, like hydrangea, have just one leaf blade and leaf stalk.

Leaf tenants
Some insects use leaves for the development of their young. Inside each spangle gall on this oak leaf is a tiny wasp grub feeding on the gall tissue. The galls drop from the leaves in fall, and the wasps then develop into adults.

Membrane
An envelope made up of two membranes surrounds and protects the chloroplast.

Granum

Light traps
A plant traps light and makes food inside microscopic disks called chloroplasts, which are inside its leaves. A sectioned chloroplast is shown in the model to the right. It is made up of flat sacs called thylakoids. Chlorophyll in the thylakoids captures light energy and this energy is used to make sugars. Sugars are used by the plant to live and grow, and oxygen is given off as a waste product. The process is called photosynthesis.

Stroma

Thylakoid
Thylakoids are made from a system of sheetlike membranes arranged neatly on top of each other. Each thylakoid is packed with chlorophyll.

How leaves breathe

A leaf has tiny mouthlike slits called stomata, named after the Greek word for mouths. The stomata are mainly on the underside of the leaf. Gases and water vapor pass in and out through the stomata. A plant uses its stomata to control the rate at which it loses water.

Inside and out
Inside leaves, there are veins that carry water and minerals to the leaf and take away food made in the leaf. On the outside, a leaf has a transparent, waterproof layer on both sides.

Chlorophyll
Chlorophyll in the thylakoids absorbs blue, red, and violet light energy, and reflects green light, making leaves look green.

Starch grain
Some of the sugars produced in photosynthesis are stored as starch.

Stroma
Sugars are made in this dense, granular fluid.

Leaf structure

The hydrangea's broad leaf and branching vein pattern, seen here on both sides, are typical of a large group of flowering plants called dicotyledons, or dicots. They are called dicots because the seeds first produced by these plants have two seed leaves, unlike monocotyledons, or monocots, which have only one seed leaf.

Midrib
The large main vein of the leaf is called the midrib. In this hydrangea leaf, middle-sized veins branch off from the midrib while the rest of the leaf is crisscrossed by minor veins, or veinlets.

Introducing flowers

More than 80 percent of all living green plants have flowers. Flowering plants began to evolve during the days of the dinosaurs. The purpose of a flower is to make seeds that grow into new plants. Although flowers come in an amazing variety of shapes and sizes, they all have a similar plan. A regular flower has four parts joined to the end of a stalk and the parts are arranged in a symmetrical way. All the parts have developed from modified leaves and are arranged in four circles, called whorls. The outer circle consists of sepals, then comes a circle of petals, then one of male parts, and finally female parts. Male and female parts join to make seeds.

Saucer-shaped
This model shows the parts of a regular flower called St. John's wort. The flower is shaped like a saucer, making it easy to see the rings of modified leaves. Years ago, this flower was thought to ward off evil spirits. Today it is used to treat depression.

Black spot
Glands appear as black dots on the petals. They are characteristic of this flower family.

Yellow petal
Five colorful, wedge-shaped yellow petals attract insect pollinators.

Five spear-shaped sepals protect flower bud

Umbrellas
Flowers in the carrot family, like this hogweed, are grouped together at the same level in umbrella shapes called umbels. This arrangement makes the small flowers more obvious to passing insects and provides the insects with a landing platform. Insects carry pollen from flower to flower (pp. 16–17).

Flower structure
These tulips have six petals. They are monocots (pp. 10–11), as are grasses, palms, and orchids. Monocot flowers have parts usually divided into threes or multiples of three. Dicots, such as trees and roses, have flower parts that usually divide into fours or fives.

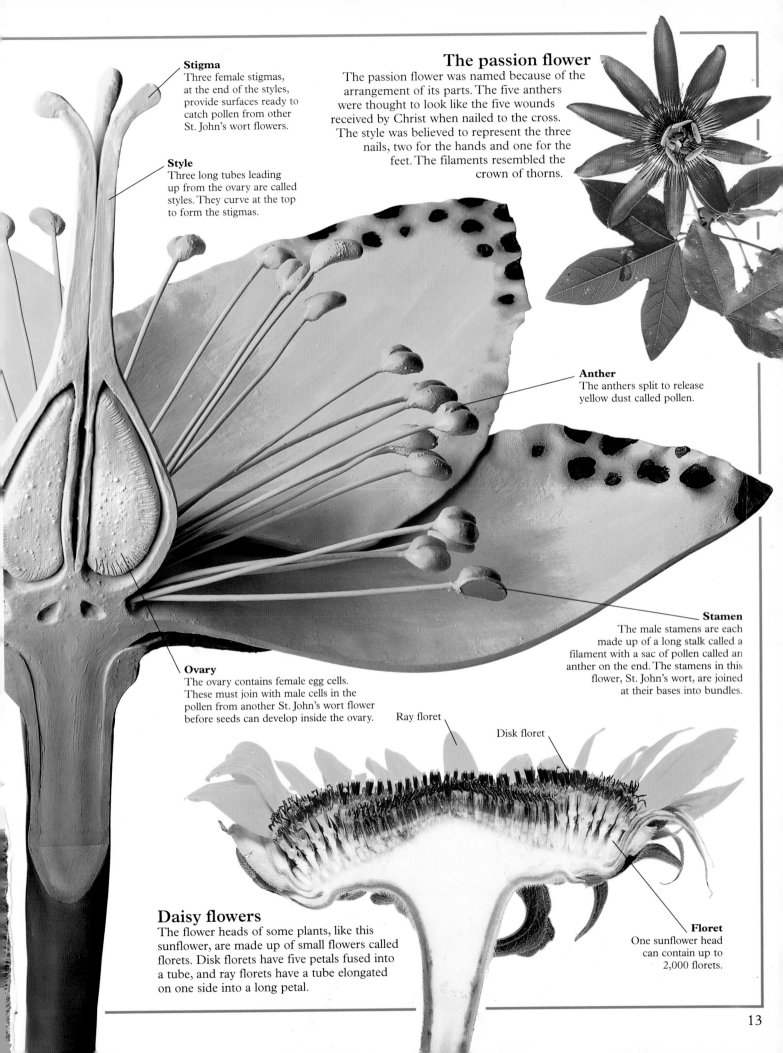

Stigma
Three female stigmas, at the end of the styles, provide surfaces ready to catch pollen from other St. John's wort flowers.

Style
Three long tubes leading up from the ovary are called styles. They curve at the top to form the stigmas.

The passion flower
The passion flower was named because of the arrangement of its parts. The five anthers were thought to look like the five wounds received by Christ when nailed to the cross. The style was believed to represent the three nails, two for the hands and one for the feet. The filaments resembled the crown of thorns.

Anther
The anthers split to release yellow dust called pollen.

Stamen
The male stamens are each made up of a long stalk called a filament with a sac of pollen called an anther on the end. The stamens in this flower, St. John's wort, are joined at their bases into bundles.

Ovary
The ovary contains female egg cells. These must join with male cells in the pollen from another St. John's wort flower before seeds can develop inside the ovary.

Ray floret

Disk floret

Daisy flowers
The flower heads of some plants, like this sunflower, are made up of small flowers called florets. Disk florets have five petals fused into a tube, and ray florets have a tube elongated on one side into a long petal.

Floret
One sunflower head can contain up to 2,000 florets.

Flower shapes

Flower parts can be arranged in all sorts of ways, and flowers of different families have different shapes. Regular flowers can be divided into two equal halves by any line drawn through the center of the flower.
The petals are usually of a similar shape, an equal distance apart, and grow out from the middle of the flower. Irregular flowers can only be divided into two equal halves one way. The two halves are usually mirror images of each other. Irregular flowers are usually of a complex shape. The different parts are not an equal distance apart, and may vary in number or size. For instance, some petals may be larger than others, or be joined to form hoods or tubes. Some parts may even be missing.

Trumpet flowers
The shapes of complex flowers are often linked to the animals that spread their pollen. Many bright-red tube-shaped flowers, like this fuchsia, are pollinated (pp. 16–17) by hummingbirds. Red is attractive to the birds.

Wolf pea
The name of this flower, lupine, comes from the Latin word for wolf. The lupine also belongs to the pea family. A pea flower has both male and female parts. They are hidden inside two boat-shaped petals called the keel, like the keel of a boat. Above the keel are two more petals called wings, and above the wings is one large, colorful petal called the standard.

Green tree frog
The green tree frog of America is in a good position to catch passing insects attracted by the bright colors of the lupine.

In a spiral
Lupine flowers are arranged in a spiral around the flower stalk.

Tall spike
Monkshood flowers grow in a tall spike above the leaves, with many flowers on each spike.

Old stamen
Old stamens bend back. Their pollen has already been released.

New stamen
New stamens bend down. They are not ready to release pollen.

Stigma
Female stigmas in the center of the flower receive pollen from another monkshood.

Ovary
The ovary is right in the middle of the flower, where it is well protected.

Inside out
A closer look inside a monkshood flower reveals the male and female parts and a large nectary standing up above them. The young stamens are bent down. Once the stamens have released their pollen, they bend back.

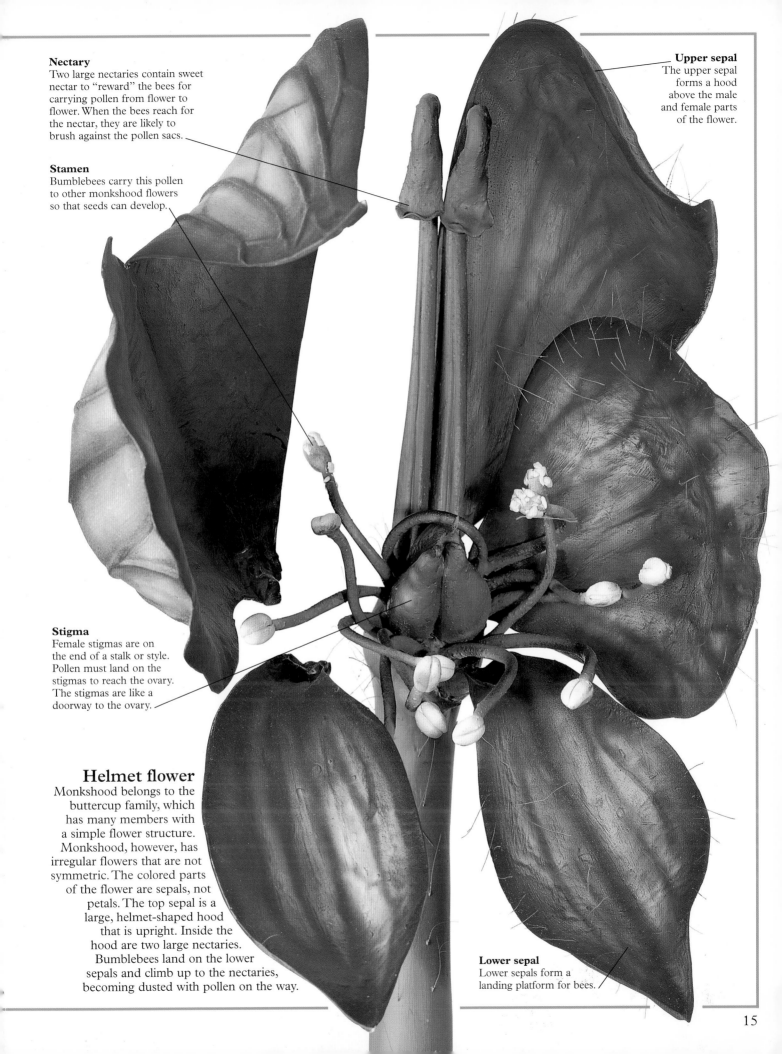

Nectary
Two large nectaries contain sweet nectar to "reward" the bees for carrying pollen from flower to flower. When the bees reach for the nectar, they are likely to brush against the pollen sacs.

Stamen
Bumblebees carry this pollen to other monkshood flowers so that seeds can develop.

Upper sepal
The upper sepal forms a hood above the male and female parts of the flower.

Stigma
Female stigmas are on the end of a stalk or style. Pollen must land on the stigmas to reach the ovary. The stigmas are like a doorway to the ovary.

Helmet flower
Monkshood belongs to the buttercup family, which has many members with a simple flower structure. Monkshood, however, has irregular flowers that are not symmetric. The colored parts of the flower are sepals, not petals. The top sepal is a large, helmet-shaped hood that is upright. Inside the hood are two large nectaries. Bumblebees land on the lower sepals and climb up to the nectaries, becoming dusted with pollen on the way.

Lower sepal
Lower sepals form a landing platform for bees.

15

Animal pollination

Insects and other animals are attracted by the bright colors and scents of many flowers. They feed on the pollen and on a sugary food made by the flowers called nectar. During their visit, the animals may accidentally pick up some pollen on their bodies. If the animals then visit another flower of the same kind, the pollen may rub off onto the stigma. The transfer of pollen from anther to stigma is called pollination. Pollination leads to the development of seeds. If flowers swap their pollen, the new plants that grow from the seeds are likely to be strong, healthy, and stand a good chance of survival.

Pollen exchange
As the bee climbs inside the flower to feed on the nectar, it brushes against the anthers and stigma, collecting and delivering pollen.

Heavyweight
Common toadflax flowers are pollinated by bumblebees, which are strong and heavy enough to push open the "mouth" of the flower. They also have long tongues to reach the nectar found at the end of a long, pointed spur.

Yellow marks
Bright yellow guide marks on the lower petal make the landing platform obvious.

Nectar
Nectar is hidden at the end of this long spur.

Pollen

4 The bee flies off with the bucket orchid's pollen stuck to his back. If he falls into the bucket of another orchid of the same species, the pollen on his back may be brushed off onto the stigma as he struggles to escape from the watery trap.

Watery liquid
Two small knobs produce a watery liquid that drips into the bucket.

Bucket orchid
The shapes and colors of orchid flowers are designed to make sure that a particular kind of insect collects and delivers pollen during its visit. The male bees that pollinate bucket orchids are enticed to the flowers by a perfume that they take from the petals and use to attract female bees in courtship.

Colorful
Bright, speckled petals help attract pollinators.

Stigma

Escaping
The bee may take 15 to 30 minutes to find his way out of the bucket.

Anther with pollen lumps attached

3 The bee squeezes through the escape tunnel, where his back catches on two lumps of the orchid's pollen. These become attached to the struggling bee's back, where they stay when he finally leaves the flower.

Bat couriers
This long-nosed bat has a long tongue with a brushlike surface to scoop up lots of nectar and pollen. Some pollen catches on the bat's head, or the front of its body, and is carried from flower to flower as it feeds.

Furry feeders
As the Australian pygmy opossum laps up the nectar from Banksia flowers, its soft fur becomes dusted with pollen. These small mammals are good at climbing to reach the flowers, but are more clumsy than insects and often damage the flowers.

Pocket
The bees take perfume from the petal and store it in pockets on their back legs.

1 When a bucket orchid flower opens, liquid drips down into the bucket. It collects to form a pool. The flower then gives off a strong smell. The perfume attracts male euglossine bees, which scrape off droplets of the oily, liquid perfume with their front feet.

2 While collecting perfume, a male bee sometimes slips and falls down into the bucket. He swims around in the liquid, but cannot climb up the sides of the bucket or fly out. Eventually, he discovers the only escape route, a narrow opening in the front wall of the bucket.

Pollen journeys

Many flowering plants in cold, wet, and windy climates, where there are few insects, use the wind to carry their pollen. Wind-pollinated plants, such as trees and grasses, often grow together in large numbers to increase the chances of their pollen blowing from anthers to stigmas. A few plants, such as pondweeds and sea grasses, rely on water to move their pollen. Pollination by wind or water is a much more haphazard process than pollination by insects or other animals.

Wind pollination

Clouds of pollen from wind-pollinated plants, such as this sedge, are one of the main causes of hay fever. The plants release huge numbers of pollen grains. Their flowers are usually small with drab colors since they do not need to attract insects. Anthers and stigmas hang outside the flower to increase the chances of pollen being blown away, and of pollen from elsewhere landing.

Sliding
Male flowers slide down the water surface into the female flower.

5 The female flower creates a little dip in the water around it. If a male flower floats near a female flower, it slides down the sides of the dip. When it bumps into the female flower, it catapults pollen over the stigmas and pollination takes place.

Ovary
The female flower is sectioned to show the ovary, filled with ovules. These will be fertilized (pp.20–21) once pollination has taken place.

Pollinated flower pulled underwater

6 Once pollen has landed on the stigmas, the flower is pulled back underwater by the flower stalk, which coils up again.

Female flower
The female flower is about 0.1–0.2 in (3–4 mm) across.

Pollen

4 When the female flower breaks through the surface of the water, it unfolds. The flower has three boat-shaped lobes, each with a fleshy stigma inside. The stigmas are covered in dense hairs that keep out the water and stop the stigmas from getting wet.

3 The female flower also forms under the water. It grows on the end of a long, bendy flower stalk that is coiled into a spiral shape at the bottom. The flower stalk straightens, pushing the flower bud up to the surface of the water. The bud opens when it reaches the surface.

Stalk
Long flower stalks grow from the base of the leaves. They are coiled up at the bottom.

Male flower
Male flowers float up to the surface like tiny divers.

2 When the male flowers are ripe, they are released from the tip of the spathe. If they are not eaten by fish, they float to the surface of the water. They have a bubble of air inside to help them float. Once the flowers reach the surface, they open out and are pushed along by the wind and water currents.

Spathe with male flowers inside

1 Ribbon weed is pollinated at the surface of the water. It has separate male and female plants. The tiny male flowers form inside a leaf-like envelope called a spathe near the bottom of the plant. Each flower has two stamens wrapped up inside three sepals.

Unopened male flowers inside leaflike envelope

Ripening fruit

7 The pollinated flower is pulled down to the bottom of the plant, where it ripens into a fruit, protected by the leaves.

Field elm pollen grain

Pollen packages

Pollen carried by the wind is as small and light as possible so that it can travel long distances. The grains often have a smooth surface since they do not need to stick onto animals. A smooth pollen grain flies faster through the air.

From pollen to seed

When pollen lands on the stigma (pp. 12–13) of a flowering plant, it is only the first step toward making a seed. A pollen tube grows out of a pollen grain, into the stigma, down the style, and into the ovary. A male sex cell travels down the pollen tube and fuses with a female sex cell stored in the ovary, creating a seed. This fusion is called fertilization. After fertilization, a baby plant starts to develop inside the seed. The ovary gets bigger and turns into the fruit, which contains and protects the seeds. Once ripe, the seeds are released by the plant or are spread by the wind, water, or animals.

Animal dispersal
Fleshy fruits may be brightly colored or have a shiny surface to attract animals such as this waxwing. Animals and birds drop the seeds, or pass the seeds out in their droppings. This moves the seeds away from the parent plant, where they are more likely to survive.

Petals
Poppy flowers have four crumpled, overlapping petals, which soon fall.

Annual flowers
Some plants, such as poppies, make seeds once and then die. They are called annuals and they survive until the next year as seeds buried in the soil. Each poppy flower can produce hundreds of seeds.

Seed capsule forms in middle of flower

Stigma and stamens
Inside the flower bud are the male stamens and the female stigma and style.

Ovules in poppy ovary

Poppy ovary
Inside this poppy ovary are the ovules waiting to be fertilized. The ovary has between eight and ten sections, or compartments.

Shaking seeds
When the fertilized seeds are ripe, the ovary forms a dry, hollow fruit with holes around the rim. As the wind blows, the ripe seeds are shaken out through the holes, like pepper out of a pepper shaker.

Ovary

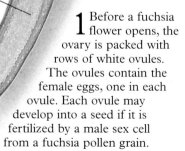

Poppy seeds
Poppy seeds are small and light, so they float easily on the wind. They usually travel only short distances, perhaps a few feet or so. They are blown farther in a strong wind.

1 Before a fuchsia flower opens, the ovary is packed with rows of white ovules. The ovules contain the female eggs, one in each ovule. Each ovule may develop into a seed if it is fertilized by a male sex cell from a fuchsia pollen grain.

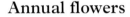

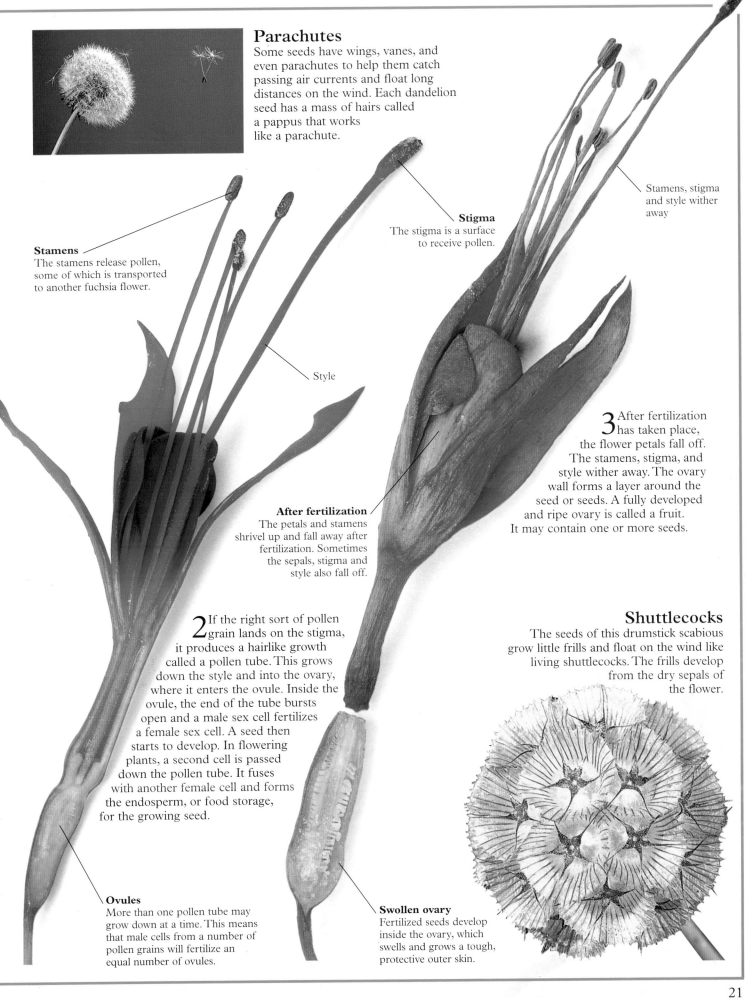

Parachutes

Some seeds have wings, vanes, and even parachutes to help them catch passing air currents and float long distances on the wind. Each dandelion seed has a mass of hairs called a pappus that works like a parachute.

Stamens
The stamens release pollen, some of which is transported to another fuchsia flower.

Stigma
The stigma is a surface to receive pollen.

Stamens, stigma and style wither away

Style

After fertilization
The petals and stamens shrivel up and fall away after fertilization. Sometimes the sepals, stigma and style also fall off.

3 After fertilization has taken place, the flower petals fall off. The stamens, stigma, and style wither away. The ovary wall forms a layer around the seed or seeds. A fully developed and ripe ovary is called a fruit. It may contain one or more seeds.

2 If the right sort of pollen grain lands on the stigma, it produces a hairlike growth called a pollen tube. This grows down the style and into the ovary, where it enters the ovule. Inside the ovule, the end of the tube bursts open and a male sex cell fertilizes a female sex cell. A seed then starts to develop. In flowering plants, a second cell is passed down the pollen tube. It fuses with another female cell and forms the endosperm, or food storage, for the growing seed.

Shuttlecocks

The seeds of this drumstick scabious grow little frills and float on the wind like living shuttlecocks. The frills develop from the dry sepals of the flower.

Ovules
More than one pollen tube may grow down at a time. This means that male cells from a number of pollen grains will fertilize an equal number of ovules.

Swollen ovary
Fertilized seeds develop inside the ovary, which swells and grows a tough, protective outer skin.

Plant beginnings

A flowering plant is born when its seed comes to life in a process called germination. Before this happens, a seed may remain dormant for weeks, months, or even years. In order to germinate, a seed needs moisture, oxygen, and the right temperature. Some seeds need a trigger to start germination, such as fire, or passage through an animal's gut.

Chinese gooseberry
The kiwi fruit is also called the Chinese gooseberry. The fruits grow on vines in the forests of China.

Kiwi

Kiwi fruits from stores are grown from pieces cut off the stem of parent plants, not from seeds. New kiwi plants are identical to their parents.

Plumule
The plumule, joined to the radicle, grows upward and eventually develops into the first shoot.

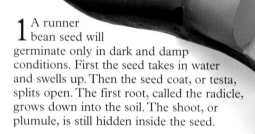

1 A runner bean seed will germinate only in dark and damp conditions. First the seed takes in water and swells up. Then the seed coat, or testa, splits open. The first root, called the radicle, grows down into the soil. The shoot, or plumule, is still hidden inside the seed.

Cotyledons
All seeds have cotyledons, or seed leaves. The runner bean has two seed leaves. They form the flesh inside the seed and are swollen with food for the developing plant.

Radicle
Tubes in the middle of the radicle carry food and nutrients taken in from the soil up to the developing shoot.

2 The plumule breaks through the seed coat and starts to grow upward, toward the light. At first it is bent in a hook shape so that the leaves are drawn up through the soil backward. This protects the delicate growing tip and the fragile leaves.

Whole lychee

Seed at center of lychee

Lychee
The lychee has a fleshy jacket called an aril around the seed. As animals eat the aril, the seed inside drops to the ground, where it begins to germinate.

Rice seedlings
Rice seedlings have to be grown in water. When they are big enough, the seedlings are gathered into bundles to be planted out in flooded paddy fields.

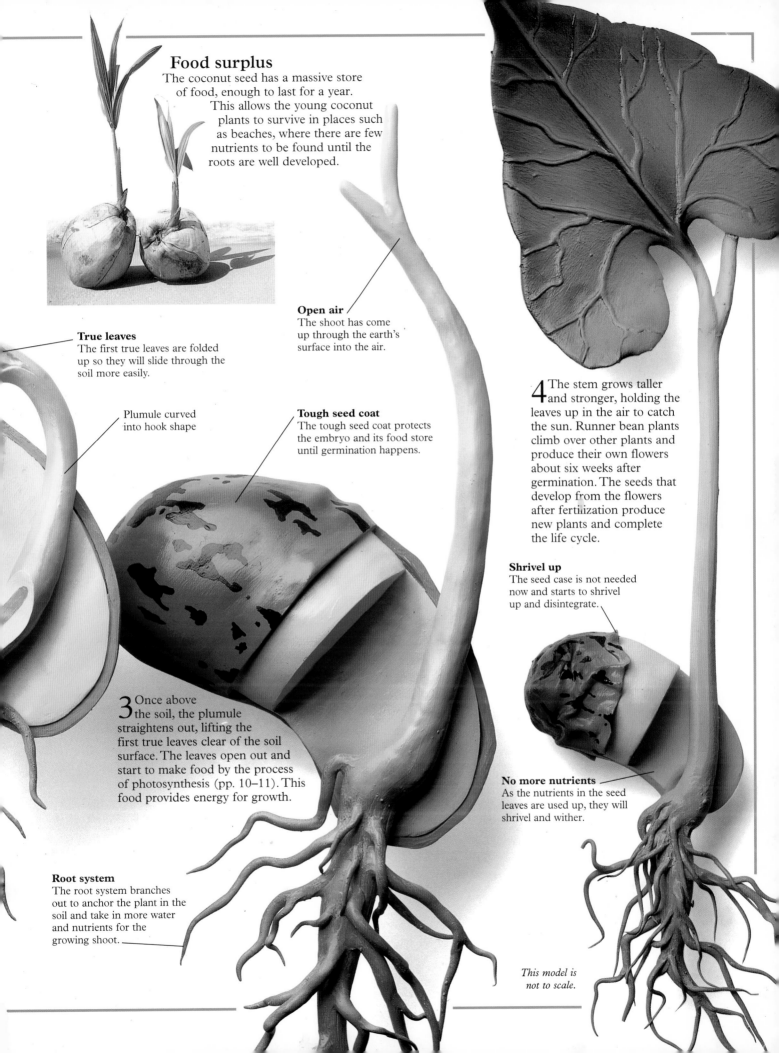

Food surplus
The coconut seed has a massive store of food, enough to last for a year. This allows the young coconut plants to survive in places such as beaches, where there are few nutrients to be found until the roots are well developed.

Open air
The shoot has come up through the earth's surface into the air.

True leaves
The first true leaves are folded up so they will slide through the soil more easily.

Plumule curved into hook shape

Tough seed coat
The tough seed coat protects the embryo and its food store until germination happens.

4 The stem grows taller and stronger, holding the leaves up in the air to catch the sun. Runner bean plants climb over other plants and produce their own flowers about six weeks after germination. The seeds that develop from the flowers after fertilization produce new plants and complete the life cycle.

Shrivel up
The seed case is not needed now and starts to shrivel up and disintegrate.

3 Once above the soil, the plumule straightens out, lifting the first true leaves clear of the soil surface. The leaves open out and start to make food by the process of photosynthesis (pp. 10–11). This food provides energy for growth.

No more nutrients
As the nutrients in the seed leaves are used up, they will shrivel and wither.

Root system
The root system branches out to anchor the plant in the soil and take in more water and nutrients for the growing shoot.

This model is not to scale.

Plants without flowers

Some plants do not have flowers or produce seeds. Plants such as ferns, mosses, liverworts, and horsetails are spread by means of small, simple structures called spores. But these plants also exist in two different forms during one life cycle. One form produces spores, the other form produces eggs and sperm. For instance, the leafy fern plant produces spores. But each spore grows into a tiny, heart-shaped prothallus, which produces eggs and sperm. A sperm has to swim through water to join an egg before a new fern plant can develop.

Spreading by spores

Ferns produce spores under their leaves in structures called sporangia. The sporangia are grouped together in clusters called sori. One cluster of sporangia is called a sorus. When the spores are ripe, the sori split open, flinging the spores out so they can drift away on passing air currents. Spores are smaller than seeds, and are good at surviving harsh conditions, such as drought or extreme temperatures.

Fern leaf

Coal forest plants

Three hundred million years ago, forests of giant horsetails as tall as trees used to cover large areas of the Earth. Their remains were buried in bogs and turned into coal. Today, most horsetails are only as tall as daffodils.

Indusium
The indusium grows out from the surface of the leaf to cover the clusters of spores.

Spore holder
Each sporangium contains 48 or 64 dark brown spores.

Fern pinna

Pinna
Each leaf has leaflets. Each leaflet is called a pinna.

Pinnule
Each pinna is subdivided into smaller pieces called pinnules.

Sori
There are six sori underneath this pinnule.

Surprise packages

Each sorus is surrounded by a thin flap called the indusium. As the sorus ripens, the indusium changes color from green to brown. Eventually it withers, revealing the sporangia underneath.

Fern pinnule

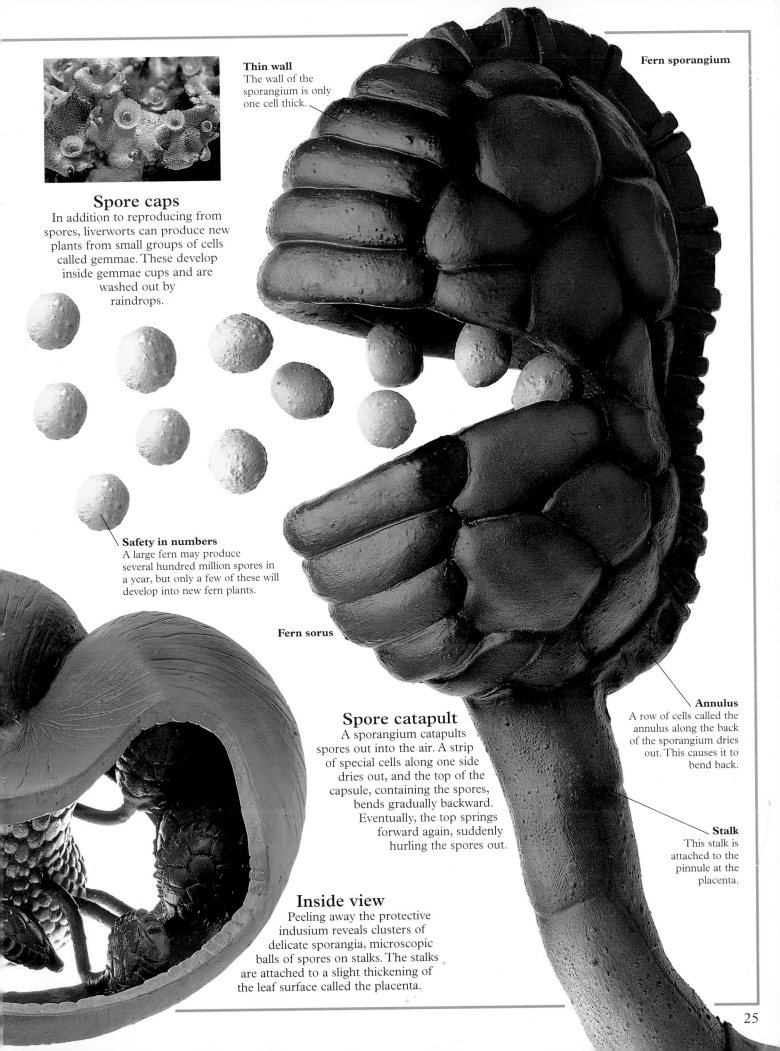

Thin wall
The wall of the sporangium is only one cell thick.

Fern sporangium

Spore caps
In addition to reproducing from spores, liverworts can produce new plants from small groups of cells called gemmae. These develop inside gemmae cups and are washed out by raindrops.

Safety in numbers
A large fern may produce several hundred million spores in a year, but only a few of these will develop into new fern plants.

Fern sorus

Spore catapult
A sporangium catapults spores out into the air. A strip of special cells along one side dries out, and the top of the capsule, containing the spores, bends gradually backward. Eventually, the top springs forward again, suddenly hurling the spores out.

Annulus
A row of cells called the annulus along the back of the sporangium dries out. This causes it to bend back.

Stalk
This stalk is attached to the pinnule at the placenta.

Inside view
Peeling away the protective indusium reveals clusters of delicate sporangia, microscopic balls of spores on stalks. The stalks are attached to a slight thickening of the leaf surface called the placenta.

Fungal spores

A fungus is more complicated than it first appears. Mushrooms or toadstools are the visible parts of fungi and hold spores, which may grow into new fungi. The rest of a fungus is hidden in the ground or the organic matter in which it grows. It is made up of a maze of branching threads called hyphae that are woven into a mat called a mycelium. A fungus has no roots, stems or leaves. Fungi cannot make their own food. Some feed on dead matter, others attack living animals and plants.

Universal veil
An outer, protective veil forms a membrane around the developing toadstool.

Sticky veil
An inner veil joins the cap to the stalk and covers the gills.

Gills

White pieces, remains of the universal veil

1 When a fly agaric toadstool reproduces, the underground hyphae join together to form a button-shaped toadstool enclosed in a protective veil. The cap of the toadstool is joined to the stalk by another, inner, veil.

Annulus
The remains of the inner veil form a ring called the annulus around the stem.

Volva, remains of the universal veil

2 As the cap expands, the universal veil splits and the cap emerges into the light. It is still rounded at this stage. Little white pieces, which are the remains of the veil, cover the cap.

Spore explosions
Pilobolus fungi produce spores in structures called sporangia that form on the end of stalks. Pressure builds up in the stalk until eventually the whole sporangium shoots off into the air. It travels for several feet. Pilobolus means "hat thrower."

Poison
Bright red color warns that this toadstool is very poisonous.

Gills
Spores are shed from vertical plates called gills that hang under the cap.

Trumpet
Bracket fungi, such as this trumpet oyster mushroom, have gills running down a short stem to one side of the cap. The spores are lilac colored.

Fire balls
Puffballs are bags that eject spores out of a hole in their tops, like a cloud of smoke. The wind carries the spores to new places. One giant puffball may produce as many as 7 million million spores.

Umbrella
The umbrella shape of the cap, or pileus, protects the delicate gills that produce the spores.

Dried up
The pieces of the universal veil dry around the edges first, causing them to curl upward.

Stalk
The stalk is made of closely packed hyphae, which branch and interlace together to create a rigid structure.

Basidia
Club-shaped structures called basidia develop from the tips of the hyphae in the gills.

Cytoplasm
A mature basidium contains a large vacuole with a narrow lining of cytoplasm.

Spore spreader
The stalk holds the cap above ground so the spores can be released into the air, helping them spread.

Nucleus

3 The fly agaric's stalk grows taller. The cap opens out into an umbrella shape and the gills hang vertically under the cap so mature spores can be dispersed. The inner veil forms a ring around the stem called the annulus.

4 The gills carry spores at all stages of development. The spores form on the tips of club-shaped structures called basidia, which are located on the edge of the gills. One toadstool may discharge as many as a million spores a minute for several days. The drier the wind is, the farther the spores will be carried.

Sterigmata
Four peglike structures called sterigmata grow from each basidium. The tip of each peg enlarges to become a spore. Each spore contains one nucleus.

Roots and stems

Roots grow downward in search of water and mineral salts found in the soil. They anchor the plant in place. Stems are above the ground. They hold the leaves up and out, toward the light. They also hold flowers in positions where wind, water, or animals can pollinate them. In shrubs and trees, the stems are woody for extra support. Smaller plants with non-woody stems rely on the pressure of the watery sap in their stems for support. Both stems and roots contain pipes through which food and water move.

New stems for old
The trunk of this tree has been cut a little way above the ground (pollarding) to encourage lots of thin, woody stems to grow for use by people.

Celery
The stringy bits in a celery stalk are the water pipes. They pass water from the soil to the leaves growing above the soil surface.

Pith
Large, soft-walled cells in the middle of the stem make up the pith.

Resin duct
Resin ducts are long, hollow tubes that produce sticky resin on their inner walls.

Xylem cells
Water travels up a stem through hollow xylem tubes.

Phloem cells
Phloem cells transport sugary nutrients up and down a stem.

Cambium layer
Cells in the cambium layer divide to produce more xylem and phloem cells.

Rings of xylem
The wood of trees, such as this pine, is mostly made up of rings of xylem cells.

Bark
Bark forms a protective outer "skin" for woody plants. It is made of corky cells.

Pine stem

Medullary ray
Rays are living channels of non-woody cells through which water and nutrients move across woody stems.

Resin duct

Stem functions
The four jobs of a stem are to support, conduct water and food, store food, and produce new living tissue.

Xylem

Pathways and pipes
In a stem, the pipes that carry water and food are usually around the outside, where they make the stem strong but also allow it to bend in the wind. The water pipes, called xylem, are made of dead cells with thick walls. The food pipes, called phloem, are made of living cells with thin walls.

Prickles
Rose thorns are actually prickles, which grow out through the outer layer of the stem, the epidermis.

Thorny skin
Non-woody stems, such as the young stems of roses, have a thick, waterproof "skin." The middle of the stem is made up of pith.

Buttercup root

Thirsty roots

Food and water pipes form the central core of a root together with packing and storage cells and the water-filled spaces around them. This arrangement makes the root tough in the middle so that it can bend and twist its way through the soil without being squashed. A protective layer of cells called the epidermis covers the outside of the root.

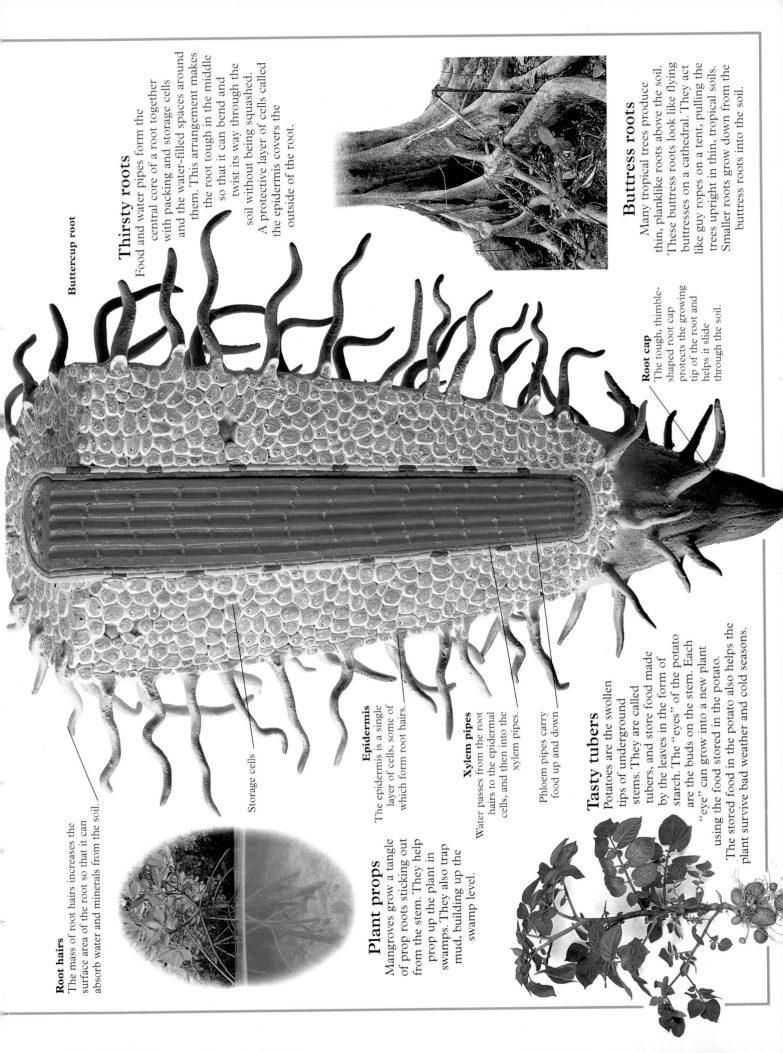

Buttress roots

Many tropical trees produce thin, planklike roots above the soil. These buttress roots look like flying buttresses on a cathedral. They act like guy ropes on a tent, pulling the trees upright in thin, tropical soils. Smaller roots grow down from the buttress roots into the soil.

Root cap

The tough, thimble-shaped root cap protects the growing tip of the root and helps it slide through the soil.

Root hairs

The mass of root hairs increases the surface area of the root so that it can absorb water and minerals from the soil.

Storage cells

Epidermis

The epidermis is a single layer of cells, some of which form root hairs.

Xylem pipes

Water passes from the root hairs to the epidermal cells, and then into the xylem pipes.

Phloem pipes carry food up and down

Plant props

Mangroves grow a tangle of prop roots sticking out from the stem. They help prop up the plant in swamps. They also trap mud, building up the swamp level.

Tasty tubers

Potatoes are the swollen tips of underground stems. They are called tubers, and store food made by the leaves in the form of starch. The "eyes" of the potato are the buds on the stem. Each "eye" can grow into a new plant using the food stored in the potato. The stored food in the potato also helps the plant survive bad weather and cold seasons.

Amazing growth

Plants grow bigger when their cells divide and expand. Some parts of a plant, such as leaves, flowers, and fruits, usually grow to a fixed size. Other parts, such as roots and stems, may keep growing throughout the life of the plant. Plant growth is slow but powerful. Most plants grow about 0.39 in (1 cm) a day, but the force of the growth is such that some plants can push their way through concrete, bricks, and asphalt. Plants have different life spans. Some live for one or two years only and grow mainly in length, while others live for many years and grow thicker as well as longer.

Record breaker
The biggest living thing in the world is one of the giant sequoia trees in California. It is called the General Sherman and is 289 ft (88 m) high, with a trunk 79 ft (24 m) wide. The wood in the tree would make 5 billion matches.

1 Sunflowers are annual plants that complete their life cycle in one growing season. They grow from seeds and send up seed leaves above the ground. These leaves grow larger and make food for the growing plant until the true leaves take over.

Flower bud
The bracts around the bud peel back to reveal the flowers inside. The "petals," which are actually individual flowers, are still tightly closed at this stage.

Bracts
At first, the buds are protected by sturdy bracts.

First leaves
The sunflower's first leaves start to make food so that the plant can grow larger.

2 Sunflower plants have to produce flowers and seeds quickly before they die. Once the plant has become established, some of the energy produced by the leaves is used to grow flowers.

Leaf growth
The leaves grow larger and wider to trap more sunlight. They are spaced to catch as much light as possible.

3 The sunflower stem grows in length, with most of the growth being concentrated in the growing tips of the roots and shoots. These tips are called meristems, and it is here that the cells keep dividing and increasing in number. Unlike animals, plants can also grow by making existing cells bigger.

Flowering spike
When ready for pollination, the flowering spike heats up and gives off a horrible smell, like rotting meat. This helps attract bees for pollination.

Spathe
The huge flowering spike, or spadix, is surrounded by a bell-shaped spathe up to 9.8 ft (3 m) across.

Fast flower
The unusual flowering structure of the titan arum grows at great speed, pushing upward at about 3.9 in (10 cm) a day. The flower, which is found in Sumatra, eventually grows 9.8 ft (3 m) tall, and yet opens for only two days. Each plant probably flowers about three times in its 20-year life span.

Old age plants
The oldest living things in the world are plants. Bristlecone pine trees in the mountains of California are more than 4,600 years old. They were alive when the ancient Egyptians were building the great pyramids at Giza.

Bulb growth

Daffodils grow from bulbs, which are made up of swollen leaf bases wrapped around a short, underground stem. A new bulb grows out from the side of an old one. The new bulb can be separated from the old one to make a new plant.

Flower head
Each of the small flowers, or florets, around the edges of the flower head has just one yellow petal.

Cultivation
The cultivated sunflowers grown as crops were developed from the wild sunflowers of Central America. The wild flowers are small, with only a few seeds, and the plants have flimsy stems.

"Petals"
The "petals" are still crumpled up and folded, but will open out to form disk-shaped flowers.

4 The flower begins to open. Its bright yellow "petals" and the nectar it produces attract various insects for pollination. Many growers place honeybee hives in their fields of sunflowers to encourage the bees to pollinate the flowers.

Stem
Sunflower stems are very strong, which is unusual for an annual plant.

Stem support
The stem supports the leaves and flowers and stops the plant from toppling over.

Sun trap
The leaves open out flat and spread wide to catch the sun.

Growing noises

It is sometimes possible to hear plants growing. Bamboo shoots may make squeaking and creaking noises as they push their way through the protective layers around the base of the shoot.

5 Sunflowers can grow up to 13 ft (4 m) tall, and probably have the tallest stems of any annual plant. After pollination, seeds develop that contain food stored as oil. Growers crush the seeds to remove oil.

Plant defense

Plants have to be very tough in order to survive. They are rooted to the spot, unable to escape the animals that eat them, so they are often protected by armor, weapons, poisons, or disguises. Many plants have spines, thorns, or stings; others rely on poisonous chemicals. Living stones are camouflaged to look like stones to deter animal and insect attackers, while mimosa plants have extra-sensitive leaves that can move around to shake off insects. Generally, plants are able to recover from an attack more successfully than most animals because they can grow new parts to replace damaged ones.

Clever camouflage
Living stones are aptly named. Their leaves are camouflaged to look like the stones they live among in the desert. Swollen leaves store water, which animals need to drink, yet the plants merge into the desert and are hard to see. Because of its ingenious camouflage, the living stone often escapes being eaten.

Matching patterns
Mottled patterns on the leaves match those on the stones around them.

Drops of poison remaining on tip of sting

Broken tip
The tip of the sting has broken off. The remaining point is sharp enough to make a hole in an animal's skin.

3 The liquid emerges through the tip of the sting partly as a result of the pressure being released, and partly because the base of the hair pushes the liquid upward. Each hair can only sting once. After stinging its victim, the sting disintegrates and falls off the plant.

Tight grip
If a nettle is gripped very firmly, the hairs are broken off near the base and the tips are unable to pierce the skin.

2 When an animal brushes against a stinging hair, the brittle tip snaps off. This exposes the upper, pointed part of the hair, which works like a hypodermic needle. The fine, stiff tube pierces the animal's skin, and the base of the hair contracts to push the poison up the hollow hair, through the tip, into the wound.

Tiny hairs
The nettle's stinging hairs are so small they can only be seen with a magnifying glass.

Tiny, glasslike bead at tip of sting

Sting top
The stinging hair tapers near the top, where the walls are thicker and stiffened with silica.

1 The nettle's stinging hair is an elongated single cell (pp. 8–9). The cell has glasslike walls and contains an irritating liquid. It has a broad, rounded base, but tapers gradually to a delicate point with a beadlike tip. When an animal is stung, the poisonous sap inside the sting produces a burning, stinging feeling and a rash.

Stinging hairs
Poisonous, needlelike stinging hairs grow out from the surface of nettles' stems and leaves. Although stings protect the nettle against larger animals, they are no defense against smaller creatures, such as butterfly caterpillars, which simply eat their way around the stings.

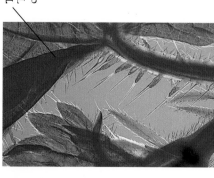

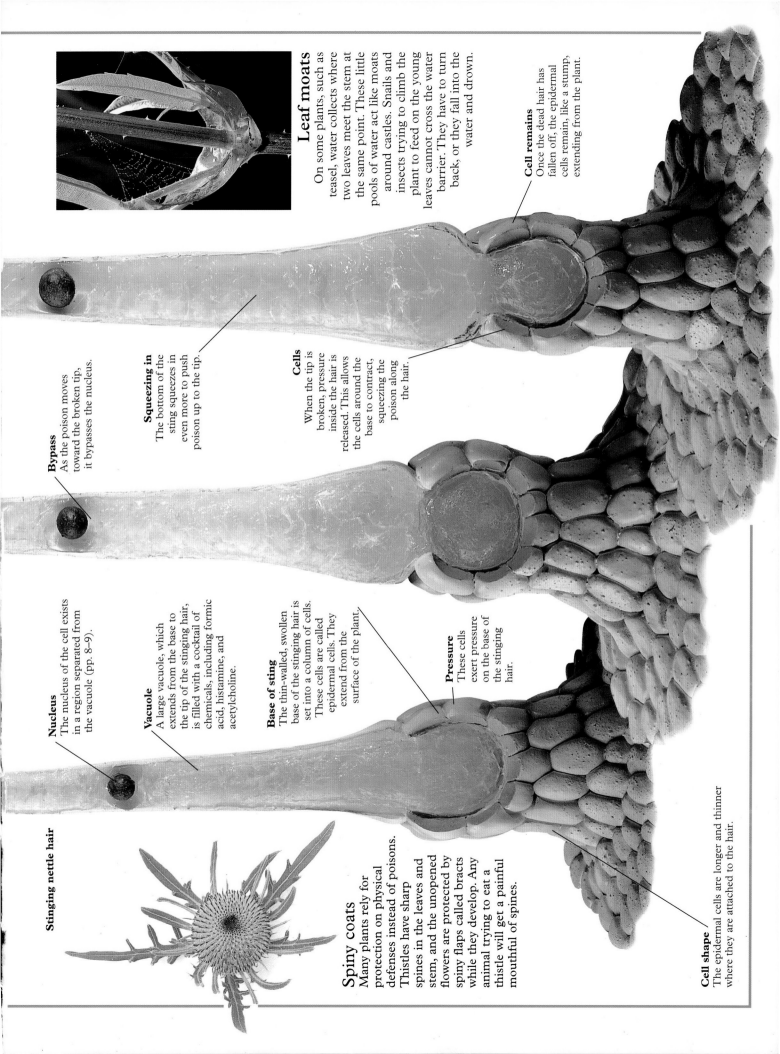

Leaf moats

On some plants, such as teasel, water collects where two leaves meet the stem at the same point. These little pools of water act like moats around castles. Snails and insects trying to climb the plant to feed on the young leaves cannot cross the water barrier. They have to turn back, or they fall into the water and drown.

Cell remains
Once the dead hair has fallen off, the epidermal cells remain, like a stump, extending from the plant.

Cells
When the tip is broken, pressure inside the hair is released. This allows the cells around the base to contract, squeezing the poison along the hair.

Squeezing in
The bottom of the sting squeezes in even more to push poison up to the tip.

Bypass
As the poison moves toward the broken tip, it bypasses the nucleus.

Nucleus
The nucleus of the cell exists in a region separated from the vacuole (pp. 8–9).

Vacuole
A large vacuole, which extends from the base to the tip of the stinging hair, is filled with a cocktail of chemicals, including formic acid, histamine, and acetylcholine.

Base of sting
The thin-walled, swollen base of the stinging hair is set into a column of cells. These cells are called epidermal cells. They extend from the surface of the plant.

Pressure
These cells exert pressure on the base of the stinging hair.

Cell shape
The epidermal cells are longer and thinner where they are attached to the hair.

Stinging nettle hair

Spiny coats

Many plants rely for protection on physical defenses instead of poisons. Thistles have sharp spines in the leaves and stem, and the unopened flowers are protected by spiny flaps called bracts while they develop. Any animal trying to eat a thistle will get a painful mouthful of spines.

Cacti and succulents

About 10,000 species of flowering plants are succulents. Succulents survive the dry conditions in which they live thanks to efficient roots to gather water and a thick "skin," or cuticle, to prevent all the water stored inside their swollen leaves, stems, or roots from evaporating. Cacti, a kind of succulent, store water in fleshy green stems. They have spines instead of leaves to minimize water loss and to protect them from plant-eating animals.

Spiny armor
The sharp leaf prickles of this agave plant help stop animals from reaching the water in its leaves.

Stem disguise
Epiphyllum cacti have flat, leafless stems that look like leaves. The stems also work like leaves, making food for the plant. In the wild, these cacti grow on rain forest trees.

Green stem
The green stem photosynthesizes since there are no leaves to make food.

Root patterns
The roots of cacti usually spread out widely in a shallow network near the soil surface. This is so that they can catch any rain that may fall. Cactus roots, such as the roots of this golden barrel, can absorb water quickly and can also take in droplets of dew that form on the plant in the early morning.

Growing up
Some roots grow up to the surface, instead of down, to catch surface moisture.

Tough skin
Tough, waxy, waterproof "skin" stops water from escaping into the air.

Leaf rosettes
Haworthias usually grow in tight rosettes of leaves close to the soil level. This helps trap moisture near the plant. The roots of haworthias can shrink to draw the plant down into the soil.

Inside a cactus
The pith in the middle of a
cactus stem is surrounded by
a ring of food and water pipes.
The rest of the stem consists
of water storage cells.

Spine
A spine is just
a leaf stalk.

Concertina stem
Many cacti have a ribbed
or pleated stem that can shrink
when dry and expand when
wet, like a concertina. This allows
the cacti to store as much water as
possible when it does rain. Up to 90
percent of the weight of a cactus is water.

Animal traps

In places with poor soil, some plants gain extra nourishment by trapping insects and other small animals with their leaves. These leaf traps range from water-filled leaves called pitchers to sticky flypaper leaves to "mousetraps" and hinged jaws. The pitcher leaves do not move, but the other leaf traps do. Plants that digest insects and animals are called carnivorous plants. They usually attract their victims with smell, color, or sugary nectar. After capturing their prey, the plants slowly dissolve the bodies with digestive juices or wait for them to decay. Then the plants soak up the precious extra nutrients into their leaves.

Leaf tip
Pitchers develop from leaf tips that grow into tendrils, then swell and fill with air.

Inside the pitcher
Once inside the pitcher, the insects either decompose or are digested.

Quick disposal
A pitcher takes a few days to dispose of a large insect, but a small midge may be eaten up in hours.

Meal in a jug
Pitcher plants are like pitfall traps. Insects are attracted by scent or color to the pitcher. Then they slide down the walls and drown in water or digestive juices.

Sticky drops
Drops of a sticky substance both trap and digest small insects.

Arching hairs
The fly's movement makes the sticky hairs of the sundew arch over it.

Fly in sticky hair trap

1 Sundew leaves have special hairs with drops of sticky "glue" on the ends. Insects are attracted to the glistening drops and stick to them like flies stick to flypaper in people's homes. The leaves of this plant are 1.18 in (3 cm) long. Another kind of sundew, from Australia, has leaves up to 2 ft (60 cm) long. It attracts and catches frogs.

2 As the fly struggles to free itself, the hairs on the sundew leaf are stimulated to curl around its body. A hair bends with amazing speed. It can turn 180° in less than a minute. This movement is produced by each hair growing on one side only, making it bend over. The sundew then has its meal firmly glued in place and trapped inside a cage of sticky hairs.

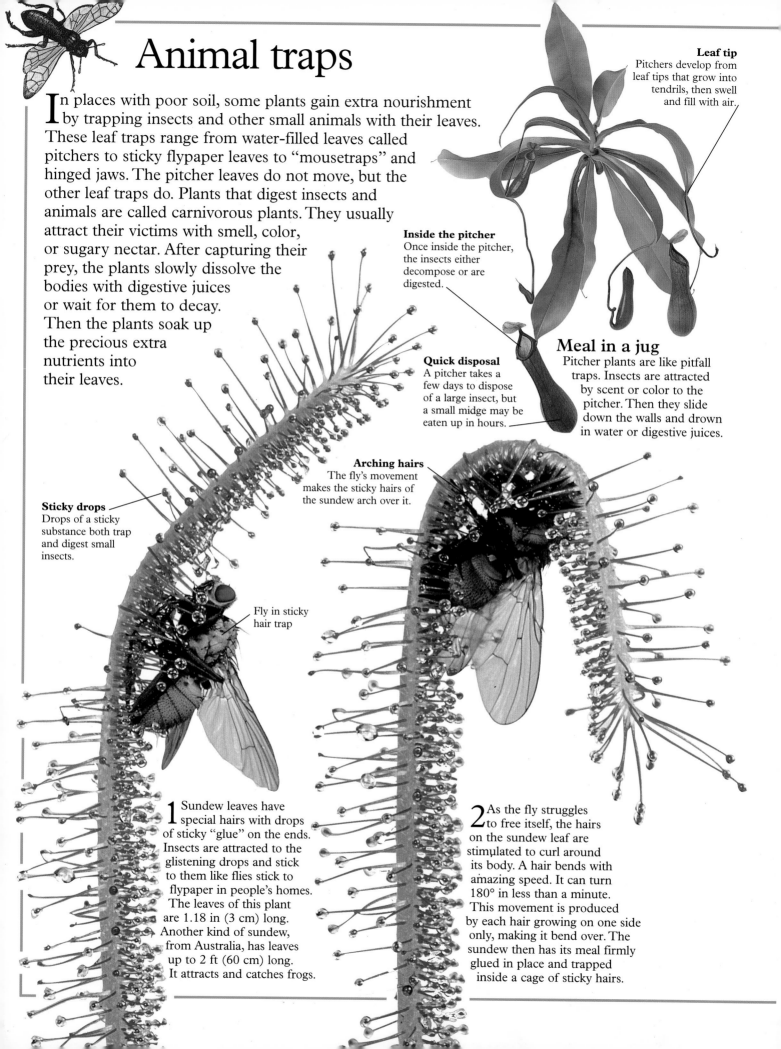

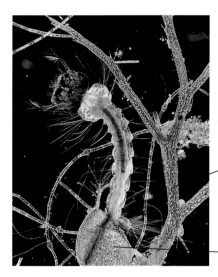

Mousetraps

Underwater bladderworts have small sacs on thin, feathery leaves. These sacs have a trapdoor with a trigger hair. The slightest movement of the trigger causes the door to snap open. Water is sucked into the space, carrying with it any passing creature.

Jaws of death

If an insect lands on the leaf of a Venus's-flytrap and touches more than one hair, or one hair more than once, the two lobes of the leaf snap shut in about one-third of a second. Small insects may crawl out through the spikes on the leaves, but larger insects are doomed. The lobes crush the insect's body and acidic juices dissolve it into a mushy pulp.

Digestion
It takes from eight to 20 days for a Venus's-flytrap to digest an insect, depending on its size.

No roots
Bladderworts have no roots. They rely on the nutrients from their efficient traps.

Water pressure
Once the creature is caught, the pressure of the water seals the door and it is digested. The trap is never open for more than a fraction of a second.

Sweet smelling
Insects are attracted to this plant by the sweet-smelling nectar, the red color in the leaves, and the apearance of a place to land and rest.

All wrapped up
The leaf curls over the body of its prey and starts to digest it.

Straightening up
After the fly is digested, the hairs straighten out. The glue is then produced by the hairs again, enabling the sundew to catch its next prey.

3 The edges of the leaf very slowly curl around the fly's body and the hairs pour digestive juices over it. This starts to break down the meal so that it can be absorbed. A similar process of digestion goes on in an animal's stomach. Once the fly has been digested, the sundew has some of the extra nutrients it needs.

4 The fly remains in this position while its soft parts are being digested. After a day or so, all that is left of it is a dry husk, the outer casing of its body. The wind will blow this away. If the sundew's prey is larger, the whole leaf will roll up around it to strengthen the trap. In this case, it is several days before the prey is digested.

Parasitic plants

About one percent of all flowering plants – several thousand kinds – steal all their food from other plants. They are called parasites, and the plants they grow on are called hosts. Many parasites attach themselves to their hosts by rootlike suckers called haustoria. The haustoria grow into the host's xylem and phloem (pp. 28–29) and suck out nourishment. A few parasites live completely inside their hosts, except when they flower. Some parasites grow on a variety of different hosts, while others grow on only one kind. Half parasites can make their own nourishment, but also depend on their host for some food.

Sickly stems
Parasitic plants such as this toothwort have no green chlorophyll since they do not produce their own food. Toothwort is a parasite of hazel or elm trees.

Haustoria
The cells inside the haustoria die off, leaving a hollow "straw" through which the dodder sucks water and food from its host.

Dodder threads
Threads grow out of the dodder and push their way through the host's cells.

Dodder stems
Threadlike stem of dodder wraps around stem of host plant.

Dependent
Dodder plants are totally dependent on their host plant and cannot live a separate life.

Suffocating
Dodders produce branching networks of many thin, thread-like stems that can sometimes cover their host completely. Young dodders have roots, but these wither away once the parasite begins to suck food from its host and no longer needs it from the soil.

Vampire suckers
Dodder stems wrap tightly around the host plant's stem. When the two plants touch, the dodder sends out suckers called haustoria at every possible place. The haustoria push their way into the xylem and phloem and suck out water and nutrients.

Tree passengers

Mistletoe grows on branches of trees from apples and poplars to larches, pines, and firs. The germinating seeds put out haustoria, which worm their way into the tree to seek out the xylem and phloem.

Plant spongers

Mistletoe has green leaves to make some food for itself, but it also takes food from its tree host. The sticky berries are often lodged into trees by birds.

Growing
Once the haustoria reach the xylem and phloem, they grow bigger and develop woody walls.

Haustoria

Stem
Haustoria are produced only if the dodder stem touches the host's stem.

Spiraling
Dodder stems spiral in the air and are attracted by chemicals given off by the host.

Fusing
Haustoria fuse to the xylem and phloem of the host.

Host plant
Dodders are parasitic on a wide variety of plants from alfalfa, ivy, heather, and clover to nettles, hops, and many tropical trees.

Surprise flower

The biggest flower in the world is produced by the rafflesia parasite, which grows on vines in Borneo and Sumatra. Its flower can be 36 in (91 cm) in diameter. The plant usually lives inside vine roots.

Living together

Some plants develop special partnerships with other living things, from bacteria, algae, and fungi to ants and wasps. In many of these partnerships, the plant has creatures living inside its body, but plants may also live inside animals. The plants and the other living things help each other survive. Ants are particularly common plant partners. They may defend the plant, or provide it with food in return for a safe place to nest.

In search of light
This ant plant is an epiphyte, perching on a forest tree to get closer to the light. It cannot take in nutrients from soil.

Leathery leaves
The shoot has leathery leaves and, at certain times of year, small white flowers.

Healthy leaves
The leaves of the ant plant are healthy. They flourish because the ants have provided the plant with the phosphates and nitrates that it needs.

Abscission
A hole, called an abscission, in the stem remains after one of the leaves has fallen off.

Perching ivy
Ivy plants climb up trees to get closer to sunlight. They have woody climbing stems that cling to the tree trunks with extra roots called adventitious roots. These grow along the ivy stems to provide extra anchorage. Plants like ivy that live on the surface of other plants without taking water or food from them are called epiphytes.

Spreading seeds
Ants also help spread the seeds of this plant.

Fair exchange
The ants provide the plant with extra food and the plant gives the ants food and a safe home.

Algae
The green patches are groups of algae living inside the clam.

Plants inside animals
Millions of tiny green plants called algae live inside giant clams. They survive in a space between the clam's soft body and its hard shell and are exposed to the light when the clam opens the two halves of its shell. The algae feed on some of the clam's waste products while, in return, the clam feeds on some of the algae.

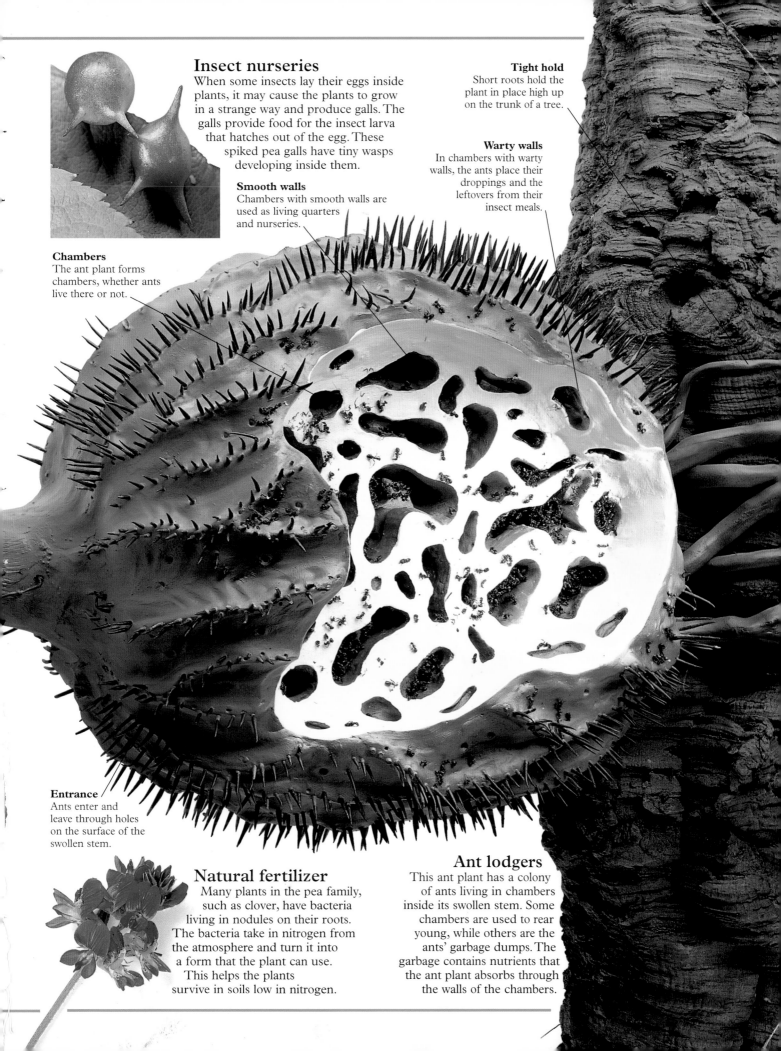

Insect nurseries
When some insects lay their eggs inside plants, it may cause the plants to grow in a strange way and produce galls. The galls provide food for the insect larva that hatches out of the egg. These spiked pea galls have tiny wasps developing inside them.

Tight hold
Short roots hold the plant in place high up on the trunk of a tree.

Warty walls
In chambers with warty walls, the ants place their droppings and the leftovers from their insect meals.

Smooth walls
Chambers with smooth walls are used as living quarters and nurseries.

Chambers
The ant plant forms chambers, whether ants live there or not.

Entrance
Ants enter and leave through holes on the surface of the swollen stem.

Natural fertilizer
Many plants in the pea family, such as clover, have bacteria living in nodules on their roots. The bacteria take in nitrogen from the atmosphere and turn it into a form that the plant can use. This helps the plants survive in soils low in nitrogen.

Ant lodgers
This ant plant has a colony of ants living in chambers inside its swollen stem. Some chambers are used to rear young, while others are the ants' garbage dumps. The garbage contains nutrients that the ant plant absorbs through the walls of the chambers.

Glossary

A

Algae
A varied group of plants, or plant-like organisms, with no roots, stems, or leaves, living in water or in damp places.

Anther
The part of a flower stamen that produces pollen.

Fly agaric toadstool

C

Cambium
A layer inside roots and shoots that contains cells that keep dividing and growing. It produces xylem from one side and phloem from the other side.

Camouflage
A disguise that helps hide a plant from animals that might eat it. It usually involves colors, patterns, or shapes that blend with the plant's surroundings.

Cell
The smallest living unit. Plants are built of cells with rigid cell walls.

Cellulose
A kind of sugar plants make and use as a building material.

Fern sporangium

Chlorophyll
A pigment inside chloroplasts that captures light energy for photosynthesis.

Chloroplast
A microscopic sac in most green plant cells in which photosynthesis takes place.

Cotyledon
The first leaf or leaves of a seed plant, found in the seed. Some cotyledons store food and stay below ground when the seed germinates. Others open above ground.

Cytoplasm
The living contents of a cell, except for the nucleus, which are inside the cell membrane.

D

Dicotyledon (Dicot)
A flowering plant with two

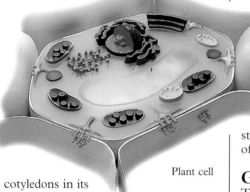

Plant cell

cotyledons in its seed. Dicots usually have broad leaves with branching veins in a netlike pattern.

E

Embryo
A young developing plant inside a seed.

Epidermis
The outer layer of cells in stems and leaves.

Epiphyte
A plant that grows on the surface of other plants for support, but does not take water or food from them.

F

Fertilization
The joining together of special male and female cells to make a new living plant. Male cells are in pollen grains and female egg cells are in ovules.

Filament
Any threadlike structure, such as the stalk of a flowering plant stamen.

Fern sorus

Floret
A small individual flower within a flower head.

Fruit
The ripe ovary of a flower containing seeds. Fruits can be either fleshy and juicy or hard and dry.

G

Gall
An abnormal growth on a plant stem or leaf, that is caused by the activity of insects, fungi, or bacteria.

Germination
The process in which a new plant starts to grow from a seed or a spore.

H

Haustorium
A threadlike outgrowth of the stem, root, or hyphae of parasitic plants or fungi through which they absorb nutrients from the host.

Host
An animal or plant used by another animal or plant as a source of food.

Hyphae
Threadlike strands or filaments making up the body or mycelium of a fungus.

M

Membrane
A thin barrier around a cell controlling the substances that pass in and out.

Meristem
A zone of growth in a plant where cells divide so that the plant grows bigger. The main meristems are at the tip of each root and shoot.

Monocotyledon (Monocot)
A flowering plant with only one cotyledon in its seed. Monocots have parallel veins in their leaves.

Mycelium
The network of hyphae that make up the body of a fungus.

N

Nectar
A sweet liquid produced by flowers and some leaves to attract insects, and some birds, for pollination.

Nucleus
The control center of a cell which contains the genetic information.

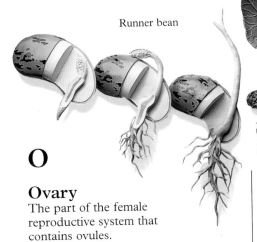

Runner bean

O

Ovary
The part of the female reproductive system that contains ovules.

Ovule
The part of the ovary in seed plants that contains the egg cell and develops into the seed after fertilization. There are usually several ovules in an ovary.

P

Parasite
A plant that obtains its food from another species, the host, usually harming the host in some way.

Petal
A modified leaf, often brightly colored, that joins with others to form a ring inside the sepals of a flower. Colored petals help attract animal pollinators.

Phloem
The living food pipes in plants through which sugary sap is carried up and down to all parts of the plant.

Photosynthesis
The process by which green plants use the Sun's energy to turn carbon dioxide gas and water into sugars, plant food.

Pith
A mass of spongy packing cells often found in stems.

Plumule
The developing shoot of a plant embryo, made up of a short stem and young leaves.

Pollen
Fine powder produced by anthers and male cones of seed plants. Each pollen grain contains a male sex cell.

Pollination
The transfer of pollen from the male part of a flower to the female part.

R

Radicle
The first root in a seed, produced by the embryo.

S

Seed
A structure consisting of an embryo and a food store, called the endosperm, surrounded by a protective coat called a testa.

Sepal
The leaflike outer parts of a flower that protect the bud.

Sorus
A cluster of sporangia in ferns, fungi, mosses, and algae.

Sporangium
A structure that makes spores in ferns, fungi, mosses, and algae. More than one sporangium are called sporangia.

Spore
A small reproductive structure of a fern, fungus, moss, or alga, which is capable of growing into a new plant. Spores are usually made up of one cell and are not the result of fertilization.

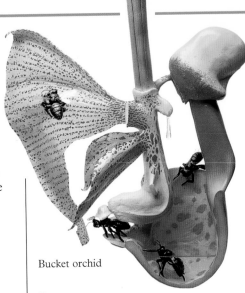

Bucket orchid

Stamen
A structure that makes pollen in a flowering plant. A stamen is made up of a stalk or filament with sacs of pollen called anthers on the end.

Stigma
A structure that receives pollen and is usually connected to the ovary by a stalk called the style.

T

Tuber
A rounded swelling at the end of an underground root or shoot.

X

Xylem
A system of water pipes in plants made up of rows of dead cells joined end to end. Xylem carries water and minerals upwards, from roots to leaves.

Pine stem

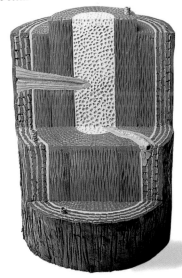

Index

Acknowledgments

The publisher would like to thank: The Linnean Society and the Royal Botanic Gardens Kew for providing reference material.

Editorial assistance: Julie Ferris, Nicki Waine

Design assistance: Emma Bowden, Goldberry Broad, Carlton Hibbert, Iain Morris, Kati Poynor

Additional photography: Steve Gorton, Kim Taylor

Photographic assistance: Sarah Ashun, Dave Morgan, Caroline Williams

Photoshop retouching: Bob Warner

Picture Credits:
Key: t=top; b=below; c= center; l=left; r=right
A-Z Botanical Collection Ltd.: 32 bcr;
Ardea, London: /Donald D. Burgess 20tr;
Bruce Coleman Limited: 8cl, 30br, 31tl, 38tr, 39br, /Bob & Clara Calhoun 24tr, /Alain Compo 31bl, /Kim Taylor 37tl;
Colorific: 8bl;
FLPA: /E&D Hosking 14tr, /F. Polking 13tr;
Jerry Harpur / National Trust, Erdigg: 40bl;
NHPA: /Stephen Dalton 17br, 18tr,

/Kevin Schafer 34r;
Oxford Scientific Films: 27tcr, 31tl, 33tl, /Harold Taylor Aripp 25tl, /Kathie Atkinson 17bl, /G.I. Bernard 39r, /Stephen Downer 30cl, c, cr, 3bc, br; /Michael Fogden 27tr, /Richard Kirby 9tr, /G A Maclean 21br;
Planet Earth Pictures: /P. Atkinson 29tl, / Steve Hopkin 41tl, /Norbert Wu 29br;
Science Photo Library: 30tr, /Sue Ford 22bc, /Adam Hart-Davis 21tl;
Tony Stone Images: /Michael Busselle 28tr, /Darrell Gulin 14bl, /Rosemary Weller 12br
Every effort has been made to trace the copyright holders. DK apologizes for

any unintentional omissions and would be pleased, in such cases, to add an acknowledgement in future editions.

Index: Marion Dent